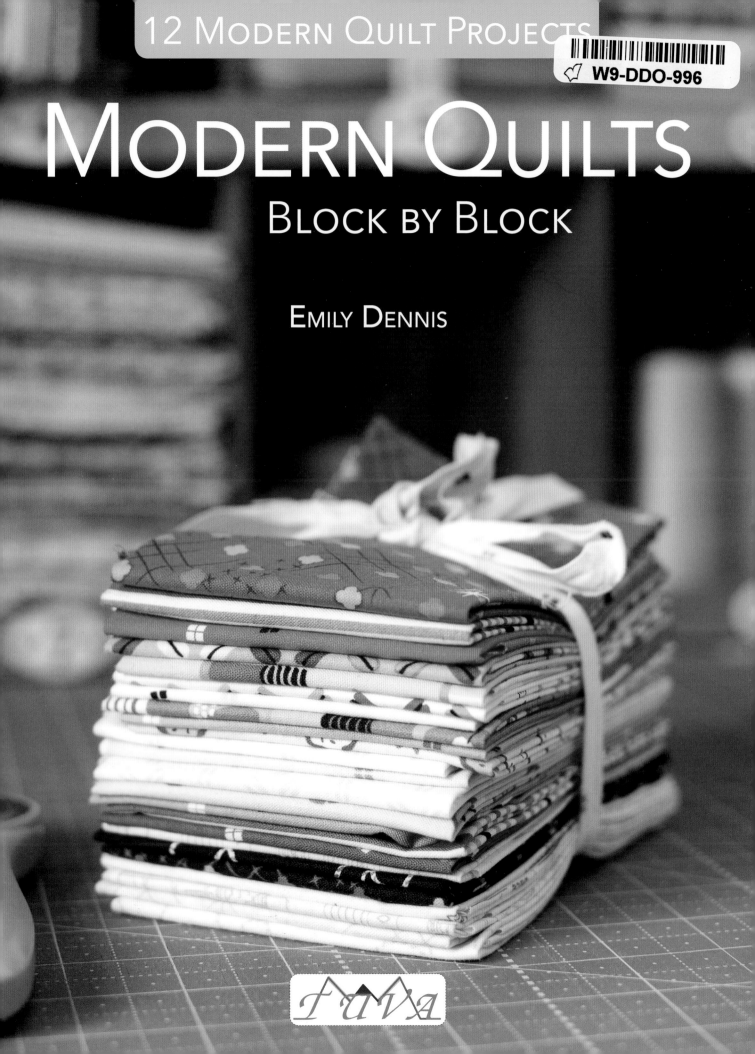

MODERN QUILTS
BLOCK BY BLOCK

EMILY DENNIS

Tuva

Tuva Publishing
www.tuvapublishing.com

Address Merkez Mah. Cavusbasi Cad. No:71
Cekmekoy - Istanbul 34782 / Turkey
Tel: +9 0216 642 62 62

Modern Quilts Block by Block

First Print 2018 / September

All Global Copyrights Belong To
Tuva Tekstil ve Yayıncılık Ltd.

Content Quilting

Editor in Chief Ayhan DEMİRPEHLİVAN
Project Editor Kader DEMİRPEHLİVAN
Designer Emily DENNIS
Technical Editors Leyla ARAS, Büşra ESER
Graphic Designers Ömer ALP, Abdullah BAYRAKÇI,
Zilal ÖNEL
Photograph Emily DENNIS

ISBN 978-605-9192-47-7

TuvaYayincilik TuvaPublishing
TuvaYayincilik TuvaPublishing

CONTENTS

PROJECTS

INTRODUCTION

This book celebrates my love of block based quilts. I've found myself making many repeating block based quilts over the years without even realizing it. Block based quilts are versatile, easy to make and usually use smaller precuts of fabric such as fat quarters.

Many of the blocks in this book are what I like to call mix and match quilts. You start with a fat quarter bundle and each block uses 2-3 fabrics from the bundle. You can mix and match them until they are all used up.

Block based quilts are fun to design and a good place to start when thinking up your own quilt patterns. Most blocks are general sizes such as 6in, 9in, 12in or 15in. Each block can then be divided into grids making the design process simple. Not all blocks in this book follow that rule of thumb and some are unique sizes.

I like the clean crisp look of a good repeating block. They usually give your eye plenty of places to rest especially when using a neutral like white as your background fabric. You will find 11 modern quilt block designs to try out. Make each quilt individually or try each block and piece together a sampler quilt with those blocks.

Modern Quilts Block by Block is for any skill level of quilter. Once you learn the basics of quilting you should be able to tackle any project in this book.

I believe quilts are meant to be used and loved. Let go of your perfectionism when it comes to quilting and just enjoy the process. Quilts around here are laundered frequently and snuggled under often. The more worn and loved a quilt becomes, the better.

PROJECT GALLERY

Page 16

Page 22

Page 30

Page 38

Page 44

Page 52

Page 60

Page 66

Page 72

Page 82

Page 88

Page 96

ABBREVIATIONS
AND DEFINITIONS

WOF - Width of fabric

RST - Right sides together

GENERAL INSTRUCTIONS

PRESSING

When using an iron on your fabrics be sure to press them rather than iron them. Press by lifting the iron when you move it rather than sliding it across the fabrics. Sliding an iron across fabrics can cause the fabrics to stretch and warp. Use the steam feature on your iron to get nice flat seams.

NEST SEAMS

When you press your fabrics in opposite directions they will nest together in the final assembly. This creates more accurately pieced blocks and faster construction as less pinning is required. Nest seams as shown through the instructions or feel free to press seams open and pin instead.

TOOLS AND MATERIALS

Sewing Machine
Rotary Cutter
Cutting Mat
Rotary cutting rulers such as a 6½in x 24½in
Seam Ripper
Iron and Ironing board
Straight pins
50wt thread
Fabric
Scissors
1/4in foot
Sewing Needles

FABRIC PREPARATION

All patterns in this book assume fabric is unwashed and all widths of fabric are at least 42in. If you prewash your fabric you may need a little extra yardage to account for shrinking. If you always prewash your fabrics, go for it! Just be sure to give them a good press before cutting into them.

I prefer not to prewash my fabrics because I like working with them while they are still crisp from the manufacturer. I'm willing to take the risk of bleeding fabrics in the end. I do however always wash my quilts for the first time with a color catcher or two.

SEAM ALLOWANCES

All patterns in this book assume a 1/4in seam allowance. An accurate 1/4in seam is an important quilting technique. Getting an accurate seam allowance will ensure your blocks come out the correct size. Practice your 1/4in seam on scrap fabrics or using an index card with 1/4in lines.

A 1/2in seam allowance is recommend when piecing backings together.

Backstitching is not necessary when seam lines are crossed by another seam. You may find it necessary to backstitch on edges that will not be crossed over.

DIRECTIONAL PRINTS

The patterns in this book do not take directional fabrics into consideration. If you use directional fabrics you may require a little extra yardage than the patterns call for. I rarely worry about the direction of directional fabrics since I don't mind them going every which way in my quilts.

PROJECTS

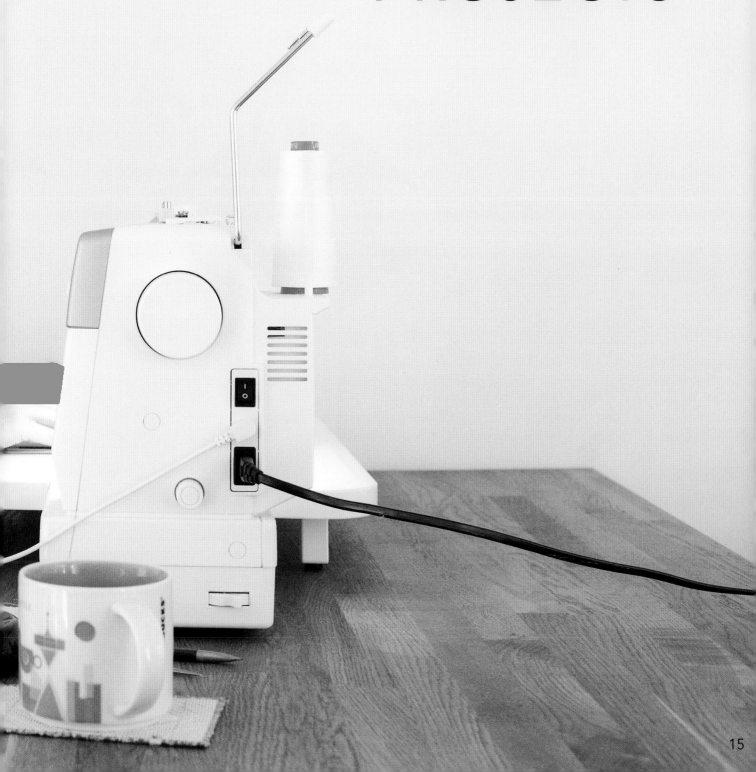

Churn Dash

Grab ten of your favorite fat quarters and mix and match them for this fun and playful quilt. Churn Dash is a traditional quilt block made up with bold corner units.

THROW SIZE
58IN X 72IN
20 BLOCKS | 12IN BLOCK

MATERIAL REQUIREMENTS

- Solid Fabrics x10 fat quarters
- White Fabric 3½ yards
- Binding Fabric ⅝ yard
- Backing 3⅔ yard
- Batting 66in x 80in

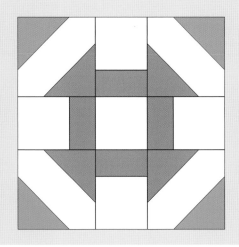

CUTTING INSTRUCTIONS

FROM EACH FAT QUARTER

- Cut x16 3½in squares
- Cut x8 2in x 3½in

FROM BINDING FABRIC

- Cut x7 2½in x WOF strips

FROM THE WHITE FABRIC

- Cut x9 3½in x WOF

Subcut x100 3½in squares

- Cut x10 5in x WOF

Subcut x80 5in squares

- Cut x1 12½in x WOF

Subcut x15 2½in x 12½in

- Cut x12 2½in x WOF

Set aside for sashing

FAT QUARTER CUTTING DIAGRAM 21IN X 18IN

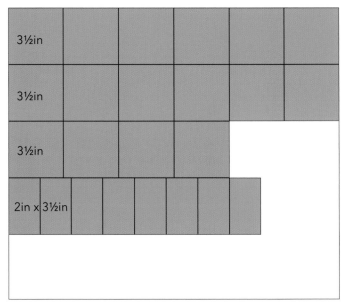

Cuts for 2 blocks

18

MIX AND MATCH THE FABRICS

✎ Mix and Match the pieces for each block. / Each block needs the following fabric cuts:

BACKGROUND

✎ x5 3½in squares

✎ x4 5in squares

COLOR A

✎ x4 3½in squares

COLOR B

✎ x4 3½in squares

✎ x4 2in x 3½in

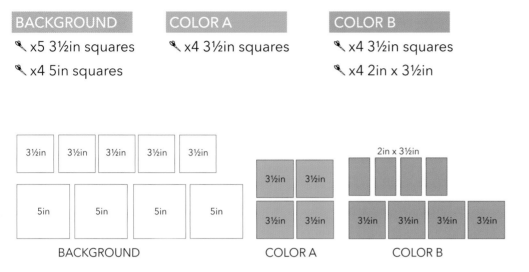

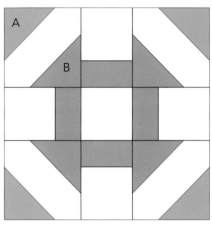

MAKE THE CORNER UNITS

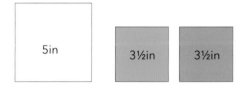

✎ Make the corner triangle units using one background 5in square, one 3½in (A) square and one 3½in (B) square.

✎ Mark a diagonal line on the wrong side of each 3½in A square and each 3½in B square.

✎ Place an A square on the background square RST as shown.

✎ Sew on the marked line.

✎ Trim ¼in from the marked line.

✎ Flip corner open and press.

✎ Repeat in the opposite corner with the B square.

✎ Repeat for all four corners.

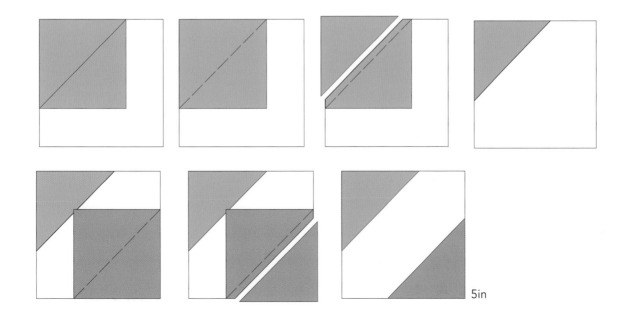

ASSEMBLE THE BLOCKS

✎ Sew four 2 x3½in (B) rectangles to four 3½in background squares.

✎ Sew the quilt block together in rows.

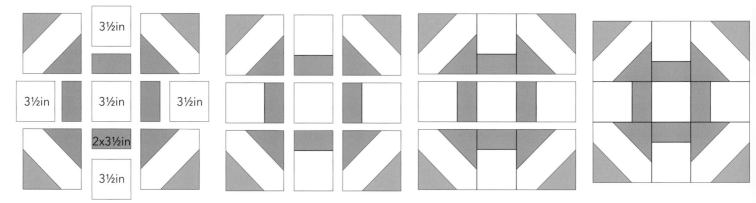

ASSEMBLE THE QUILT TOP

✎ Arrange the quilt blocks in five rows of four. Add 2½in x 12½in sashing pieces between blocks.

✎ Sew together all of the sashing WOF strips end to end. Cut to each row length of 54½in.

✎ Sew rows together adding the sashing in between each row and the top and the bottom.

✎ Cut the side sashing to 72½in. Attach to both sides.

Figure Eights

Figure eights is made up of large bold rectangle blocks in a shape that reminds me of figure eights. This modern geometric design is a fun one to sew up. Use just nine ⅓ yard cuts and make nine sets of blocks.

THROW SIZE
60½IN X 72½IN
18 BLOCKS | 12IN X 18IN

MATERIAL REQUIREMENTS

- Solid Fabrics x9 ⅜ yards
- White Fabric 2¼ yards
- Binding Fabric ⅝ yards
- Backing Fabric 3⅞ yards
- Batting 68in x 80in

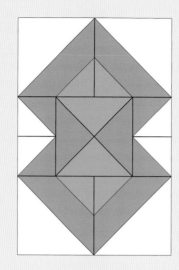
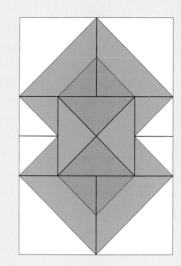

CUTTING INSTRUCTIONS

FROM EACH SOLID FABRICS

- Cut x2 10in squares
- Cut x2 7¼in squares
- Cut x8 3½in squares
- Cut x2 5½in square

FROM BINDING FABRIC

- Cut x7 2½in x WOF strips

FROM THE WHITE FABRIC

- Cut x5 10in x WOF

Subcut x18 10in squares

- Cut x3 5½in x WOF

Subcut x18 5½in squares

- Cut x1 9½in x WOF

Subcut x3 9 ½in x 12 ½in Cut x1 additional

9 ½in x 12 ½in piece from piece from extra fabric.

CUTTING DIAGRAM 42IN X 13.5IN (WOF FOLDED IN HALF)

WOF folded in half

MIX AND MATCH THE FABRICS

Pair up colors so you have 6 sets of blocks.

Each block needs:

- ✎ x1 10in white square
- ✎ x1 5½in white square
- ✎ x1 10in print square - Fabric A
- ✎ x1 5½in print square - Fabric A
- ✎ x1 7¼in print square - Fabric A
- ✎ x4 3½in print squares - Fabric B
- ✎ x1 7¼in print square - Fabric B

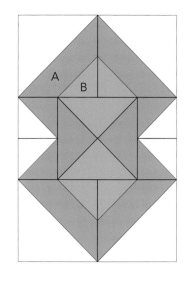

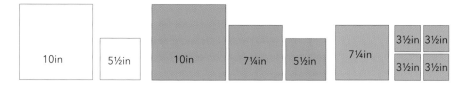

MAKE THE HOURGLASS UNITS

✎ Make the center hourglass units using one 7¼in (A) square and one 7¼in (B) square.

✎ Place the squares RST.

✎ Mark a diagonal on the wrong side of the fabric.

✎ Sew ¼in away from the marked line on each side.

✎ Cut on the marked line.

✎ Press the units open towards the darker fabric.

✎ Place the two half square triangles right sides together in opposite directions. The seams should nest.

✎ Mark a line on the diagonal that's perpindicular to the seam line. Pin in place to prevent shifting.

✎ Sew ¼in on each side of the drawn line.

✎ Cut on the marked line.

✎ Press units open. Makes two hour glass units.

✎ Trim to 6½in.

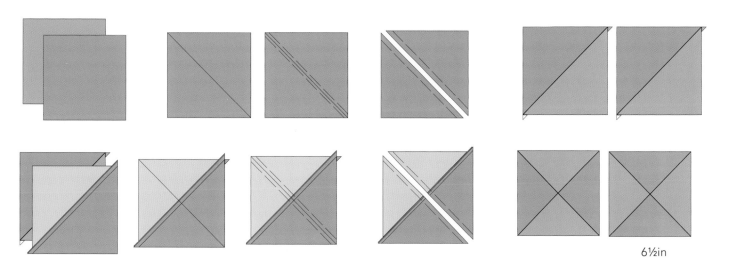

6½in

MAKE THE LARGE HALF SQUARE TRIANGLES - FOUR AT A TIME

✎ Make the half square triangles four at a time.

✎ Place a 10in (A) square and a 10in background square right sides together. Pin in place and sew ¼in around the outside of the square.

✎ Cut the sewn unit on each diagnol.

✎ Press half square triangles open. Press seams open or towards the darker fabric.

✎ Trim to 6½in square.

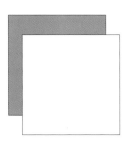  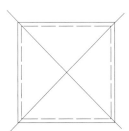 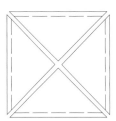 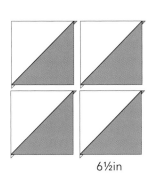

6½in

MAKE THE SMALL HALF SQUARE TRIANGLES - FOUR AT A TIME

✎ Repeat the same steps above this time using one 5½in background square and one 5½in (A) square.

✎ Trim to 3½in square.

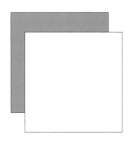  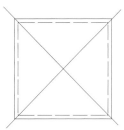 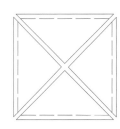 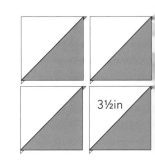

3½in

MAKE THE CORNER SQUARE TRIANGLES

✎ Make the corner triangle units using the 6½in half square triangle and a 3½in (B) square.

✎ Mark a diagnol line on the wrong side of the 3½in B square.

✎ Place an A square on the background square RST as shown.

✎ Sew on the marked line.

✎ Trim ¼in from the marked line.

✎ Flip corner open and press.

✎ Repeat for all four corners of the block.

6½in

ASSEMBLE THE BLOCK

✎ Sew together the smaller half square triangles.

✎ Assemble the block in rows. Press as shown.

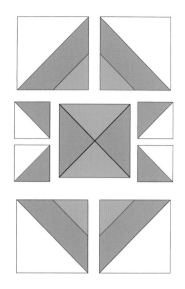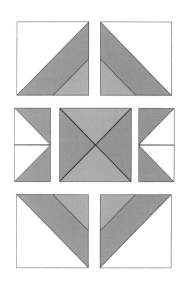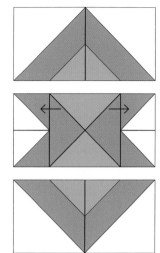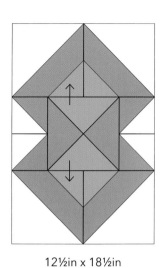

12½in x 18½in

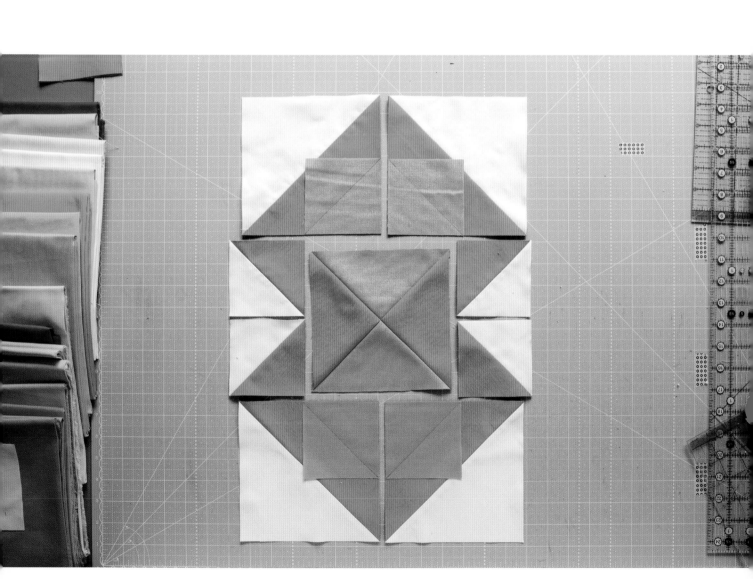

ASSEMBLE THE QUILT TOP

✎ Arrange the quilt blocks in columns adding the background pieces in as shown.

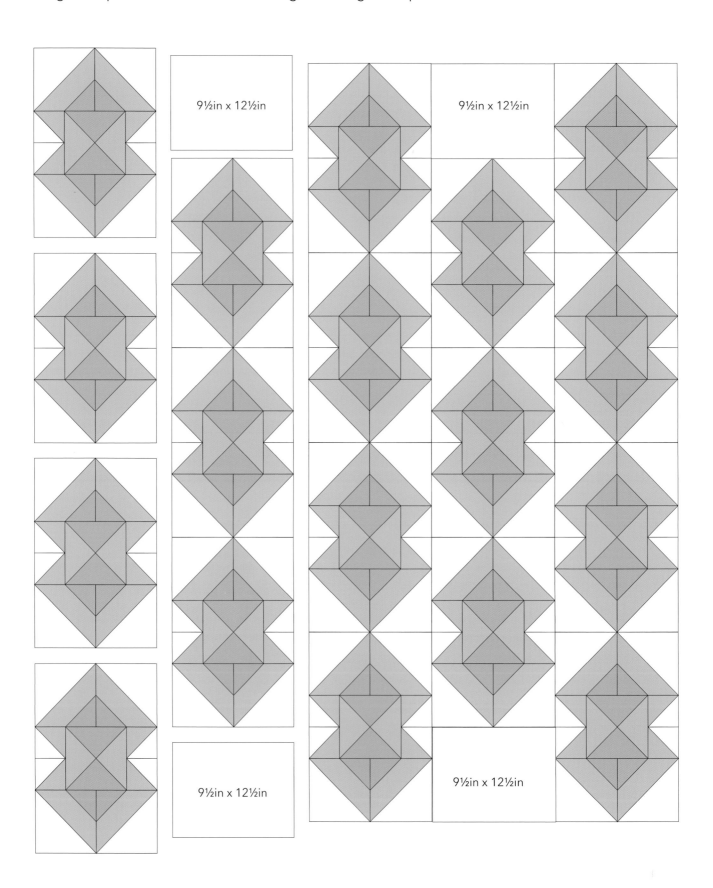

First Place

First Place reminds me of a ribbon you might get at the county fair. Choose an accent that is subtle or bold to show off the spotlight fabrics. This one is sure to be a showstopper using your favorite fabrics.

THROW SIZE
60IN X 75IN
20 BLOCKS | 15IN BLOCK

MATERIAL REQUIREMENTS

- ✎ **Solid Fabrics** 20 Fat Eighths
- ✎ **Accent Fabric** 2 yards
- ✎ **White Fabric** 2⅓ yards
- ✎ **Binding Fabric** ⅝ yard
- ✎ **Backing** 3⅞ yard
- ✎ **Batting** 68in x 83in

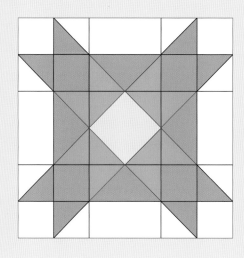

CUTTING INSTRUCTIONS

FROM EACH FAT EIGHTH

- ✎ Cut x2 3¾in squares
- ✎ Cut x4 3⅜in squares

FROM THE ACCENT FABRIC

- ✎ Cut x6 3in x WOF strips

Subcut x80 3in squares

- ✎ Cut x4 6¼in x WOF

Subcut x20 6¼in squares

- ✎ Cut x5 4¾in x WOF

Subcut x40 4¾in squares

FROM BINDING FABRIC

- ✎ Cut x7 2½in x WOF strips

FROM THE WHITE FABRIC

- ✎ Cut x5 4¾in x WOF

Subcut x40 4¾in squares

- ✎ Cut x6 5½in x WOF strips

Subcut x80 3in x 5½in

- ✎ Cut x6 3in x WOF

Subcut x80 3in squares

- ✎ Cut x2 4in x WOF

Subcut x20 4in squares

FAT EIGHTH 21IN X 9IN

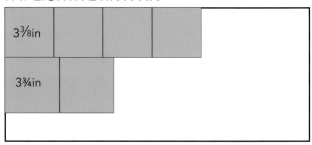

MIX AND MATCH THE FABRICS

✎ Mix and Match the pieces for each block.
Each block needs the following fabric cuts:

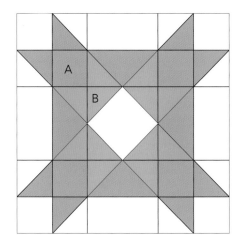

BACKGROUND	COLOR A	COLOR B
✎ x4 3in x 5½in	✎ x4 3in squares	✎ x2 3¾in squares
✎ x4 3in squares	✎ x1 6¼in square	✎ x4 3⅜in squares
✎ x1 4in square	✎ x2 4¾in squares	
✎ x2 4¾in square		

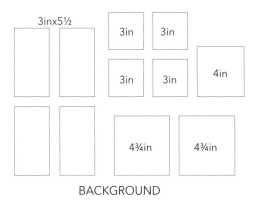

BACKGROUND

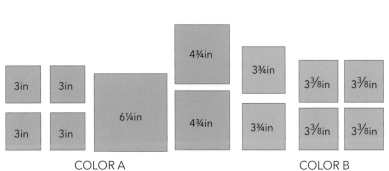

COLOR A   COLOR B

MAKE THE HALF SQUARE TRIANGLES - FOUR AT A TIME

✎ Make the half square triangles four at a time.

✎ Place a 4¾in (A) square and a 4¾in background square right sides together. Pin in place and sew ¼in around the outside of the square.

✎ Cut the sewn unit on each diagonal.

✎ Press half square triangles open. Press seams open or towards the darker fabric.

✎ Trim to 3in square.

✎ Make two of these units for a total of eight 3in half square triangles per block. Make 40 units for a total of eighty half square triangles for the entire quilt.

  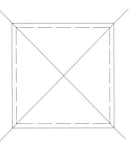 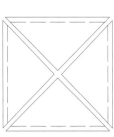 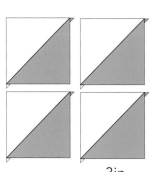

3in

MAKE THE CENTER SQUARE IN A SQUARE

   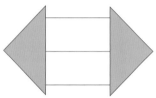

🖉 Make the center square in a square unit using one 4in background square and the two 3¾in color B squares.

🖉 Cut the 3¾in squares on the diagonal to create four triangles.

🖉 Sew the cut triangles to each side of the 4in background square. Fold the square in half to create a crease down the middle. Line the tip of the triangle up with the crease line for a perfectly centered unit.

🖉 Trim the edges straight.

🖉 Repeat on the other side.

🖉 Trim to 5½in square leaving at least ¼in between each point and the edge for the seam allowance.

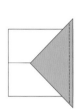 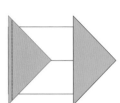 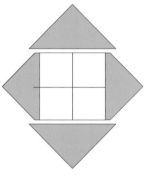 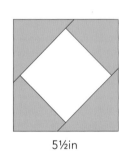

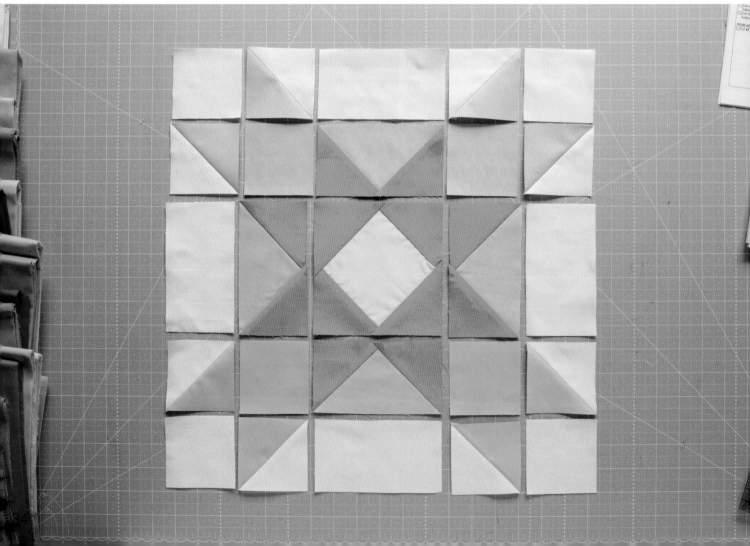

MAKE THE FLYING GEESE FOUR AT A TIME

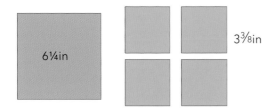

6¼in

3⅜in

🪡 Mark a diagonal line on the wrong side of each 3 ⅜in (B) square.

🪡 Place two 3⅜in squares RST on the 6¼in (A) square as shown lining up the marked line.

🪡 Sew ¼in from both sides of the marked line.

🪡 Cut on the marked line.

🪡 Flip corners up and press to form two heart shapes.

🪡 Place a 3⅜in square on each heart unit as shown.

🪡 Sew ¼in from both sides of the marked line.

🪡 Cut on the marked line.

🪡 Press the flying geese units open.

🪡 Trim to 3in x 5½in.

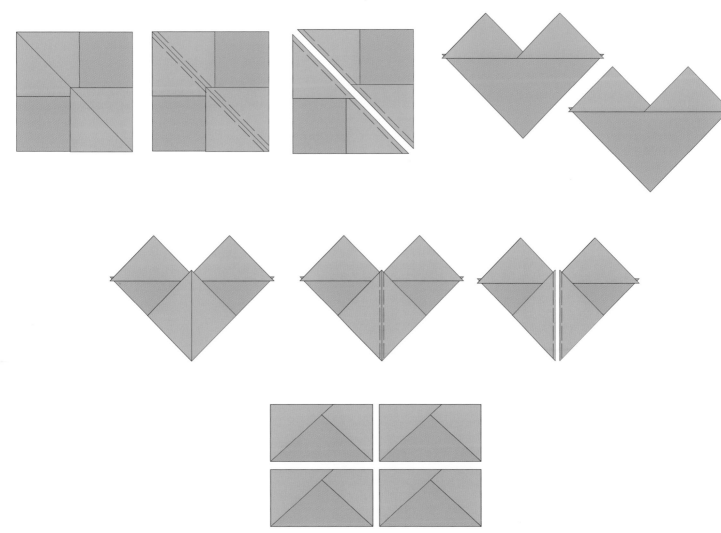

3in x 5½in

ASSEMBLE THE BLOCKS

✎ Assemble the block in rows. Press each row in opposite directions to nest the seams.

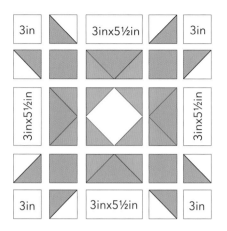 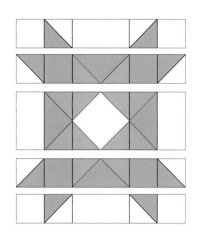 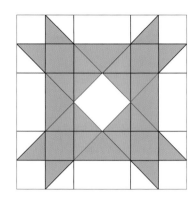

ASSEMBLE THE QUILT TOP

✎ Arrange the quilt blocks in five rows of four.

✎ Sew rows together.

Hopscotch

Hopscotch is a fun and playful lap size or baby size quilt. This single block based quilt makes a secondary repeating plus shape. Use an accent fabric that is bold or subtle and complements the main prints. Hopscotch is easy to assemble with strip piecing shortcuts.

BABY SIZE
40IN X 40IN
16 BLOCKS | 10IN BLOCK

MATERIAL REQUIREMENTS

- ✎ **Print Fabrics** x8 Fat Eighths
- ✎ **Accent Fabric** ½ yard
- ✎ **White Fabric** ⅝ yard
- ✎ **Binding Fabric** ½ yard
- ✎ **Backing Fabric** 2⅔ yards
- ✎ **Batting** 48in x 48in

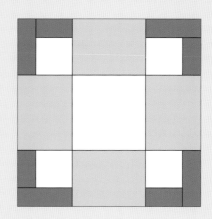

CUTTING INSTRUCTIONS

FROM EACH FAT EIGHTH

- ✎ Cut x8 3½in x 4½in

FROM THE ACCENT FABRIC

- ✎ Cut x3 3½in x WOF

Subcut x64 3½in x 1½in

- ✎ Cut x4 1½in x WOF strips

Set aside for strip piecing

FROM BINDING FABRIC

- ✎ Cut x5 2½in x WOF strips

FROM THE WHITE FABRIC

- ✎ Cut x2 4½in x WOF strips

Subcut x16 4½in squares

- ✎ Cut x4 2½in x WOF strips

Set aside for strip piecing

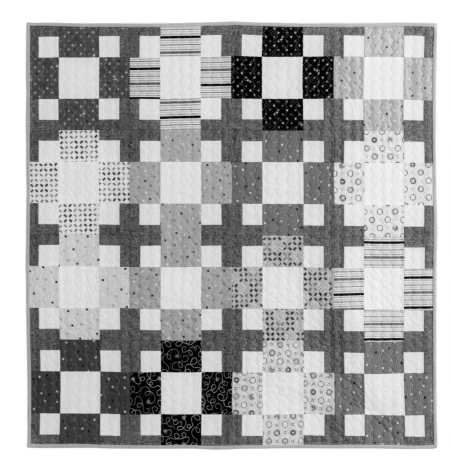

PRINT FABRICS DIAGRAM
FAT EIGHTH 21IN X 9IN

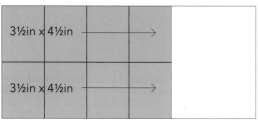

2 blocks per fat eighth

MIX AND MATCH THE FABRICS

Each block needs the following fabric cuts if making an individual block. (Follow the chain piecing cutting instructions for full quilt.)

BACKGROUND	COLOR A	COLOR B
✎ x1 4½in square	✎ x4 3½in x 4½in	✎ x4 1½in x 3½in
✎ x4 2½in squares		✎ x4 1½in x 2½in

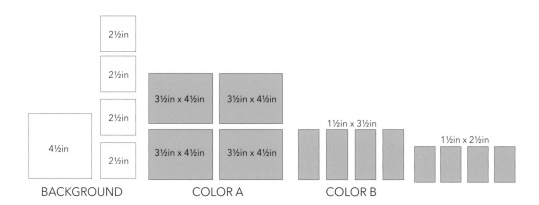

BACKGROUND   COLOR A   COLOR B

STRIP PIECING

Strip piece the corner units for faster assembly.

✎ Sew together a white 2½in WOF strip with an accent 1½in WOF strip. Press seams towards the darker fabric or open.

✎ From this new WOF cut x16 2½in wide sections.

Repeat for all strip sets for a total of x64 corner units.

✎ Sew an 1½in x 3½in accent piece to the unit.

✎ Make a total of 64 corner units.

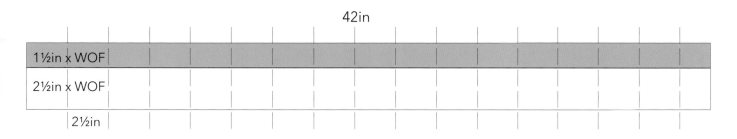

ASSEMBLE THE BLOCKS

✎ Assemble the block in rows. Press each row in opposite directions.

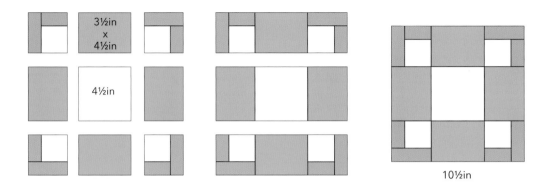

3½in x 4½in

4½in

10½in

ASSEMBLE THE QUILT TOP

✎ Arrange the quilt blocks in four rows of four rotating each block to nest seams.

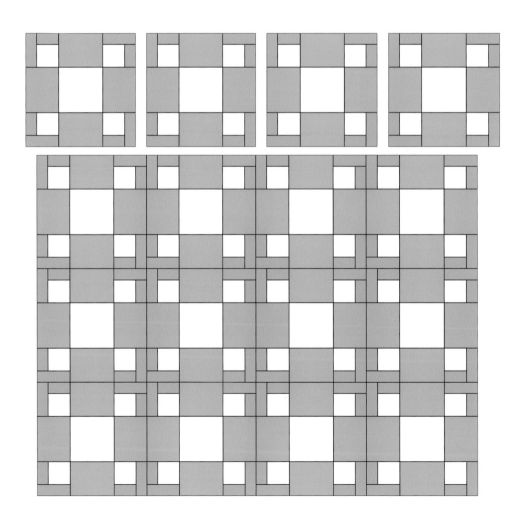

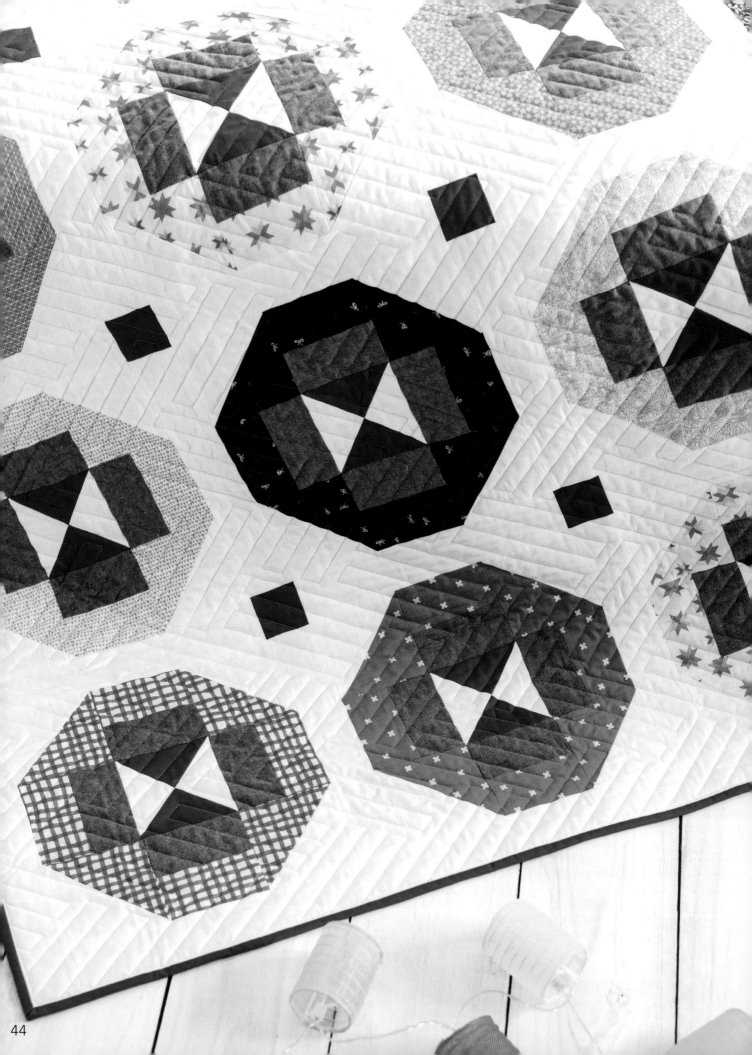

Hourglass

Choose ten of your favorite fat quarters that become the highlight of Hourglass. Show off those fabrics in this cheerful block based quilt. Choose an accent hourglass that stands out in the center of your blocks.

THROW SIZE
58IN X 72IN
20 BLOCKS | 12IN BLOCK

MATERIAL REQUIREMENTS

- Print Fabrics x20 fat eighths or 10 fat quarters
- Accent Fabric (Hourglass & cornerstones) ⅜ yard
- Accent Fabric (linen) ⅔ yard
- White Fabric 2⅓ yards
- Binding Fabric ⅝ yard
- Backing 3⅔ yards
- Batting 66in x 80in

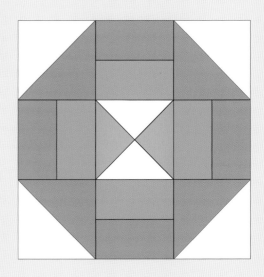

CUTTING INSTRUCTIONS

FROM EACH FAT EIGHTH

- Cut x1 7in square
- Cut x4 2½in x 4½in

(Cut double if using fat quarters)

FROM LINEN ACCENT FABRIC

- Cut x5 4½in x WOF

Subcut x80 2½in x 4½in

FROM SOLID ACCENT FABRIC (HOURGLASS AND CORNERSTONES)

- Cut x2 5¼in x WOF

Subcut x10 5¼in squares

- Cut x1 2½in x WOF

Subcut x12 2½in squares

FROM BINDING FABRIC

- Cut x7 2½in x WOF strips

FROM THE WHITE FABRIC

- Cut x4 7in x WOF strips

Subcut x20 7in squares

- Cut x2 5¼in x WOF strips

Subcut x10 5¼in squares

- Cut x2 12½in x WOF

Subcut x31 12½in x 2½in

- Cut x7 2½in x WOF

Set aside for borders

FAT EIGHTH CUTTING DIAGRAM

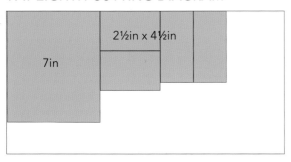

7in

2½in x 4½in

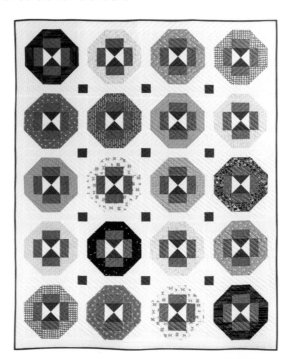

MIX AND MATCH THE FABRICS

✎ Mix and Match the pieces for each block.
Each block needs the following fabric cuts:

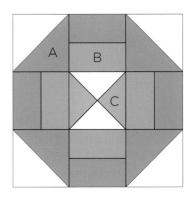

BACKGROUND	COLOR A	COLOR B	COLOR C
✎ x1 7in square	✎ x1 7in square	✎ x4 2½in x 4½in	✎ x1 5¼in square
✎ x1 5¼in square	✎ x4 2½in x 4½in		

MAKE THE HOURGLASS UNITS

✎ Make the center hourglass units using one 5¼in background square and one 5¼in (C) square.

✎ Place the squares RST.

✎ Mark a diagonal on the wrong side of the fabric.

✎ Sew ¼in away from the marked line on each side.

✎ Cut on the marked line.

✎ Press the units open towards the darker fabric.

✎ Place the two half square triangles right sides together in opposite directions. The seams should nest.

✎ Mark a line on the diagonal that's perpendicular to the seam line. Pin in place to prevent shifting.

✎ Sew ¼in on each side of the drawn line.

✎ Cut on the marked line.

✎ Press units open.

✎ Trim to 4½in.

✎ Repeat 10 times for a total of 20 hourglass units.

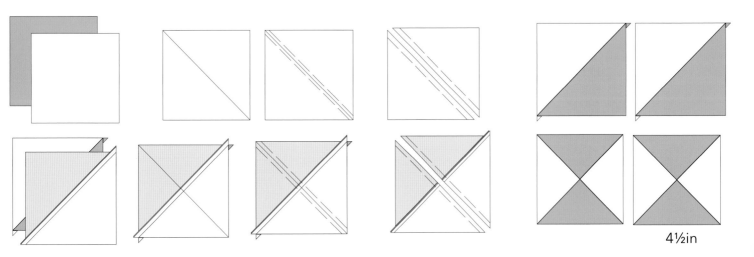

MAKE THE HALF SQUARE TRIANGLES FOUR AT A TIME

7in   7in

✎ Make the half square triangles four at a time.

✎ Place a 7in (A) square and one 7in background square right sides together. Pin in place and sew ¼in around the outside of the square.

✎ Cut the sewn unit on each diagonal.

✎ Press half square triangles open. Press seams open or towards the darker fabric.

✎ Trim to 4½in square.

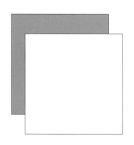  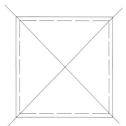 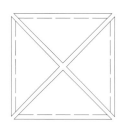 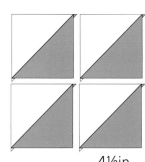

4½in

ASSEMBLE THE BLOCKS

✎ Sew together the 2½in x 4½in (A) and the 2½in x 4½in (B) rectangles RST. Press seams towards darker fabric.

✎ Assemble the block in rows. Press as shown.

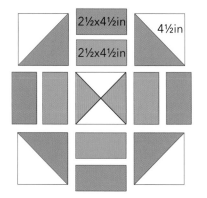 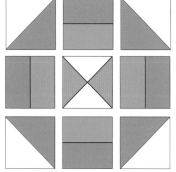 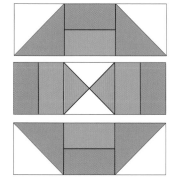 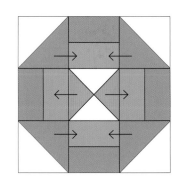

FINISH YOUR QUILT

✎ Arrange the quilt blocks in five rows of four. Add 2½in x 12½in sashing pieces between blocks.

✎ Sew together the sashing pieces with 2½in cornerstone pieces as shown.

✎ Sew rows together adding the sashing in between each row.

✎ Sew borders together end to end. Cut and attach top and bottom borders and side borders.

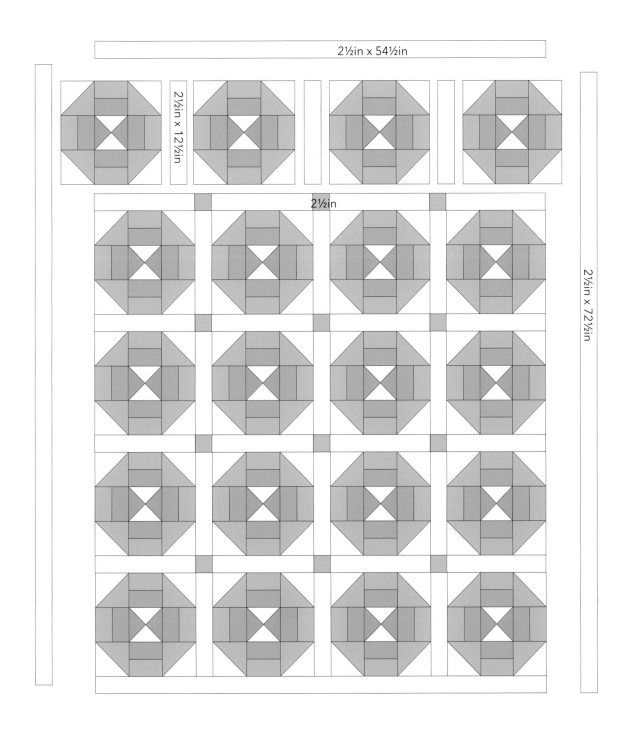

51

Kriss Cross

Kriss Cross is a bold and colorful generous throw size quilt. The blocks are large and graphic made up using half square triangles. Make this one up in bold solids or your favorite prints.

THROW SIZE
62IN X 82IN
12 BLOCKS | 18IN BLOCK

MATERIAL REQUIREMENTS

- Solid Fabrics x12 - ¼ yards or Fat Quarters
- White Fabric 2¾yards
- Binding Fabric ⅔ yard
- Backing 5 yards
- Batting 70in x 90in

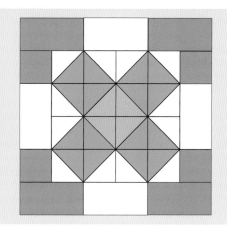

CUTTING INSTRUCTIONS

FROM EACH FAT QUARTER OR ¼ YARD

- Cut x5 5½in squares
- Cut x4 3½in x 6½in rectangles
- Cut x4 3½in squares

FROM BINDING FABRIC

- Cut x8 2½in x WOF strips

FROM THE WHITE FABRIC

- Cut x4 6½in x WOF strips
  Subcut x48 3½in x 6½in
- Cut x6 5½in x WOF strips
  Subcut x36 5½in squares
- Cut x4 2½in x WOF strips
  Subcut x8 2½in x 18½in
- Cut x11 2½in x WOF strips
  Set aside for sashing

FAT QUARTER CUTTING DIAGRAM

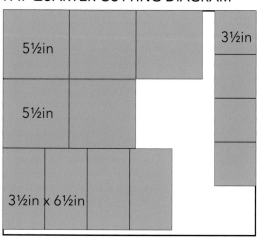

¼ YARD CUTTING DIAGRAM

MIX AND MATCH THE FABRICS

✎ Mix and Match the pieces for each block.
Each block needs:

✎ x4 background 3½in x 6½in rectangles

✎ x3 background 5½in squares

✎ x4 print or solid (A) 3½in x 6½in rectangles

✎ x4 print or solid (A) 3½in squares

✎ x4 print or solid (B) 5½in squares

✎ x1 print or solid (C) 5½in squares

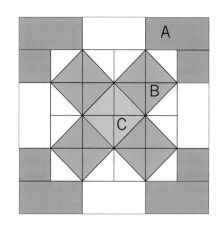

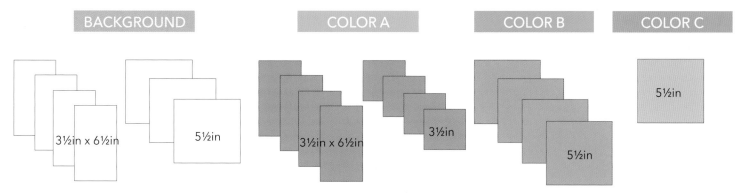

BACKGROUND — 3½in x 6½in — 5½in

COLOR A — 3½in x 6½in — 3½in

COLOR B — 5½in

COLOR C — 5½in

MAKE THE HALF SQUARE TRIANGLES - FOUR AT A TIME

✎ Make the half square triangles four at a time.

✎ Place a 5½in Color B square and a 5½in background square right sides together. Pin in place and sew ¼in around the square.

✎ Cut the sewn unit on each diagonal.

✎ Press half square triangles open. Press seams open or towards the darker fabric.

✎ Trim to 3½in square.

✎ Make three of these units for a total of twelve 3½in half square triangles per block.

✎ Repeat using one color (B) 5½in square and one color (C) 5½in square.

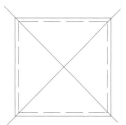

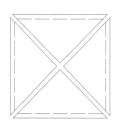

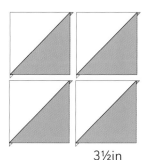

3½in

ASSEMBLE THE BLOCKS

✎ Place the half square triangles as shown. Sew together in rows. Press seams open or each row in opposite directions.

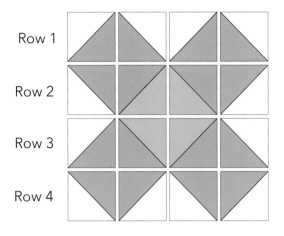

Row 1

Row 2

Row 3

Row 4

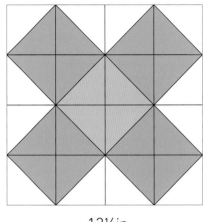

12½in

✎ Add the outside borders to the center unit as shown.

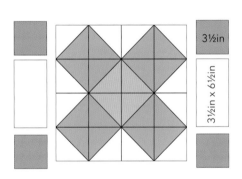

3½in

3½in x 6½in

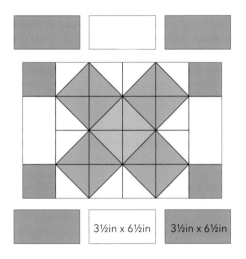

3½in x 6½in   3½in x 6½in

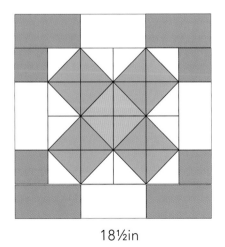

18½in

✎ Repeat for all 12 blocks.

ASSEMBLE THE QUILT TOP

✎ Arrange the quilt blocks in four rows of three. Add 2½in x 18½in sashing pieces between blocks.

✎ Sew together all of the sashing WOF strips end to end. Cut to each row length of 58½in.

✎ Sew rows together adding the sashing in between each row and the top and the bottom.

✎ Cut the side sashing to 82½in. Attach to both sides.

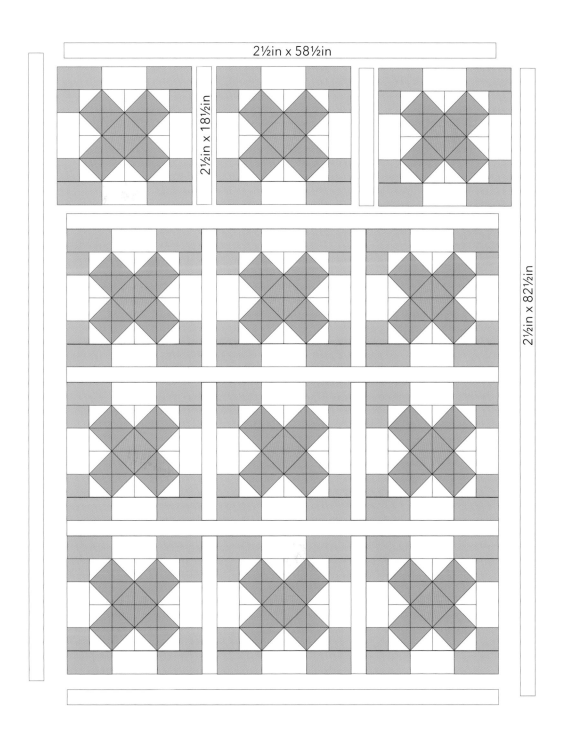

Mini Medallion

Mini Medallion is a geometric mini quilt or table topper using prints and accent fabrics. Choose a fussy cut center fabric and experiment with different accent colors.

MINI QUILT
24IN X 24IN
1 BLOCK | 24IN BLOCK

MATERIAL REQUIREMENTS

- Print or Solids Fabrics (Outer layer) 1 Fat Quarter
- Accent Fabric (Inner layer) 1 Fat Quarter
- Accent Fabric (Diamonds) 10 in square
- White Fabric 1 Fat Quarter
- Binding Fabric ¼ yard

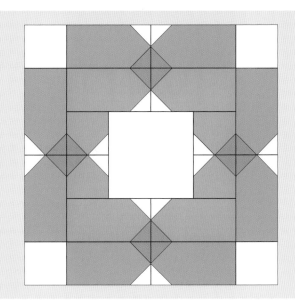

CUTTING INSTRUCTIONS

FROM THE OUTER LAYER FABRIC

- Cut x8 4½in x 8½in

FROM THE INNER LAYER FABRIC

- Cut x4 4½ x 8½
- Cut x4 4½in squares

FROM DIAMOND ACCENT FABRIC

- Cut x16 2½in squares

FROM BINDING FABRIC

- Cut x3 2½in x WOF strips

FROM THE WHITE FABRIC

- Cut x4 4½in squares
- Cut x1 8½in square
- Cut x16 2½in squares

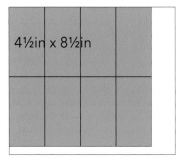

FAT QUARTER 21IN X 18IN

FAT QUARTER 21IN X 18IN

10IN SQUARE

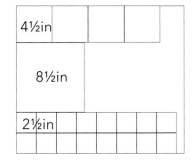

FAT QUARTER 21IN X 18IN

Each block needs the following fabric cuts:

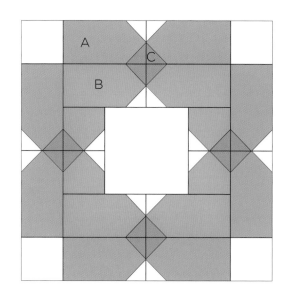

BACKGROUND
- ✎ x1 8½in square
- ✎ x4 4½in squares
- ✎ x16 2½in squares

COLOR A
- ✎ x8 4½in x 8½in

COLOR B
- ✎ x4 4½in x 8½in
- ✎ x4 4½in squares

COLOR C
- ✎ x16 2½in squares

BACKGROUND

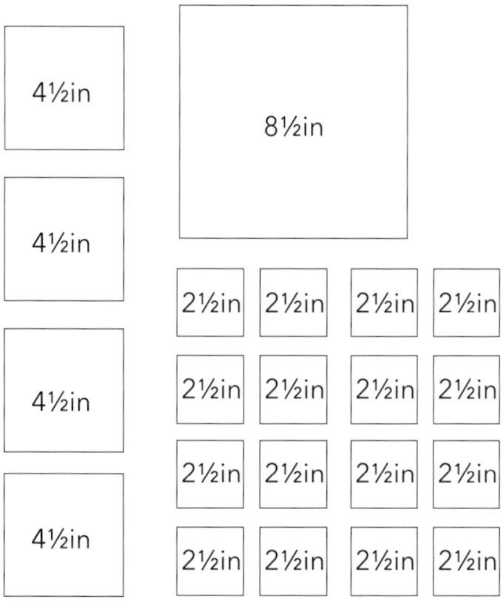

4½in	8½in
4½in	
4½in	2½in 2½in 2½in 2½in
4½in	2½in 2½in 2½in 2½in
	2½in 2½in 2½in 2½in
	2½in 2½in 2½in 2½in

COLOR A

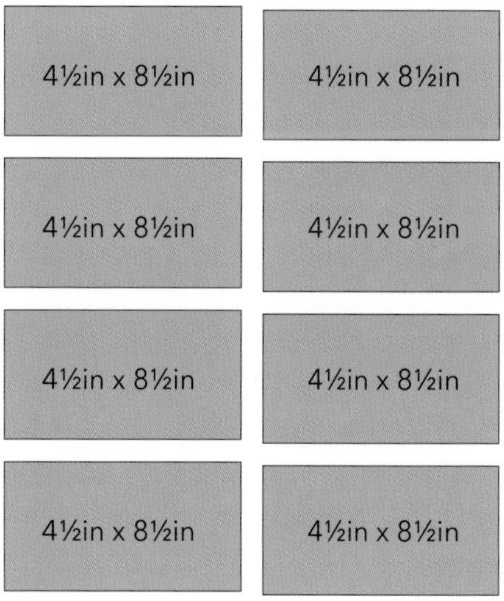

4½in x 8½in	4½in x 8½in
4½in x 8½in	4½in x 8½in
4½in x 8½in	4½in x 8½in
4½in x 8½in	4½in x 8½in

COLOR B

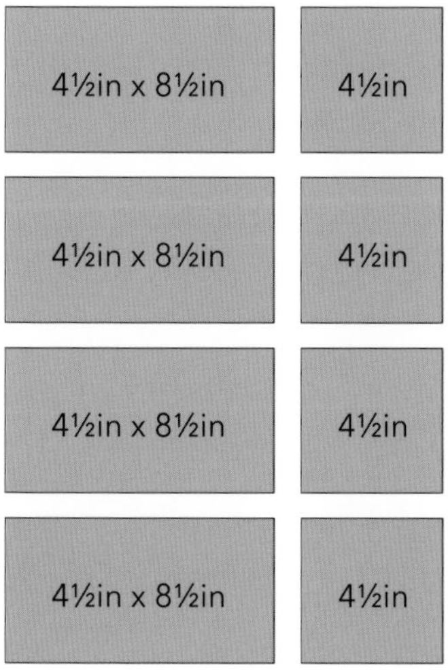

4½in x 8½in	4½in
4½in x 8½in	4½in
4½in x 8½in	4½in
4½in x 8½in	4½in

COLOR C

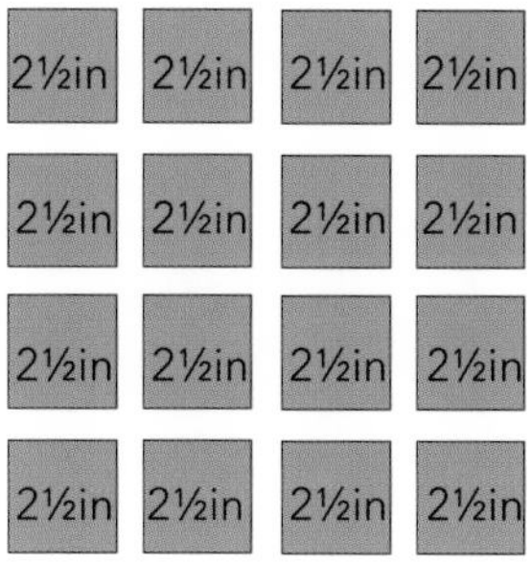

2½in	2½in	2½in	2½in
2½in	2½in	2½in	2½in
2½in	2½in	2½in	2½in
2½in	2½in	2½in	2½in

MAKE THE CORNER SQUARE TRIANGLES

✎ Make the corner triangle units using one 4½in x 8½in (A) rectangle and one 2½in background square and one 2½in (C) square.

✎ Mark a diagonal line on the wrong side of each 2½in background square and each 2½in C square.

✎ Place a background square on the (A) rectangle RST as shown.

✎ Sew on the marked line.

✎ Trim ¼in from the marked line.

✎ Flip corner open and press.

✎ Repeat in the opposite corner with the (C) squares.

✎ Make 8 units total.

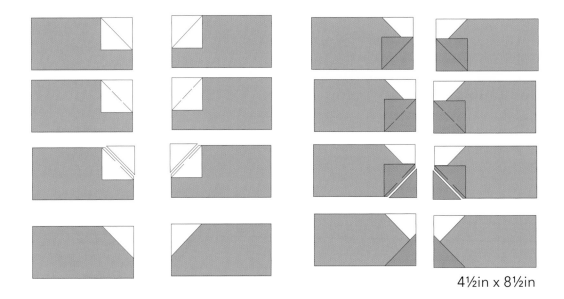

4½in x 8½in

✎ Repeat with the 4½in x 8½in (B) rectangles and a 2½in background squares and a 2½in (C) squares. Make two of the corner squares triangles on the left side and two on the right side.

✎ Make four units.

✎ Repeat with the 4½in (B) squares.

✎ Make four units total.

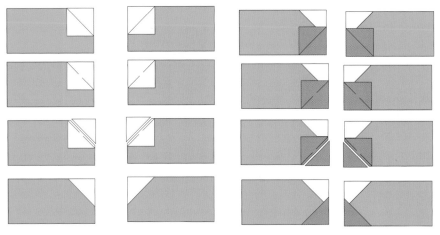

4½in x 8½in

4½in

ASSEMBLE THE BLOCK

✎ Assemble the block in rows as shown below adding the left and right side last.

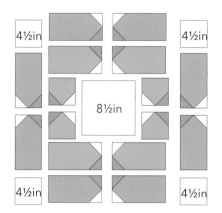

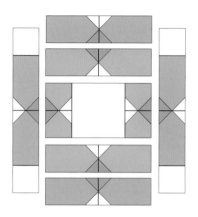

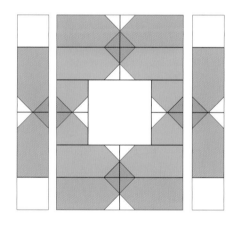

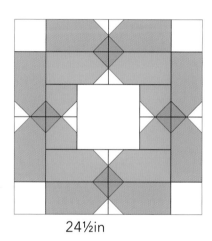

24½in

Ombre Squares

Ombre Squares is a modern plus quilt with a surprise accent. The ombre fabrics create a colorful gradient. Swap out the striped accents for polka dots or solids. Lay out your quilt blocks in an ombre gradient or randomly. Give the ombre trend a try with Ombre Squares.

THROW SIZE
63IN X 73IN
42 BLOCKS | 9IN BLOCK

MATERIAL REQUIREMENTS

- ✎ **Ombre Fabrics** x6⅓ yard cuts
- ✎ **White Fabric** 2¾ yards
- ✎ **Striped Fabric** ⅝ yard
- ✎ **Binding** ⅔ yard
- ✎ **Batting** 72in x 82in
- ✎ **Backing** 4 yards

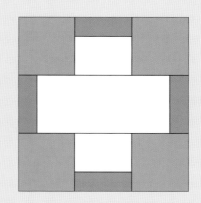

CUTTING INSTRUCTIONS

FROM EACH 1/3 YARD FABRIC

✎ Cut x3 3½in x WOF

Subcut x28 3½in squares

FROM BINDING FABRIC

✎ Cut x8 2½in x WOF strips

FROM THE WHITE FABRIC

✎ Cut x4 7½in x WOF

Subcut x42 3½in x 7½in

✎ Cut x5 3½in x WOF

Subcut x80 2½ x 3½in

✎ Cut the remaining x4 from the extra fabric above for a total of x84 2½ x 3½in

✎ Cut x2 9½in x WOF

Subcut x35 1½in x 9½in

✎ Cut x9 1½in x WOF

Set Aside for sashing

✎ Cut x7 2½in x WOF

Set aside for borders

FROM THE STRIPED ACCENT FABRIC

✎ Cut x6 3½in x WOF

Subcut x168 1½in x 3½in

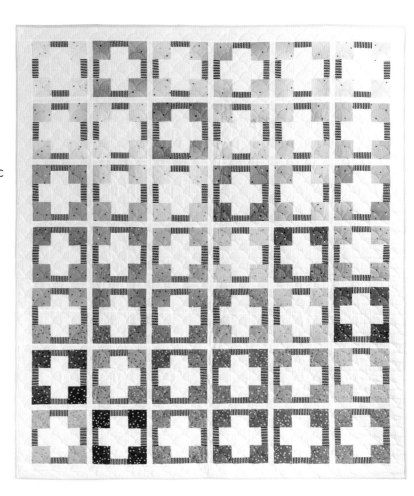

MIX AND MATCH THE FABRICS

✎ Mix and Match the pieces for each block.
Each block needs the following fabric cuts:

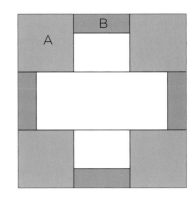

BACKGROUND
✎ x1 3½in x 7½in

✎ x2 2½in x 3½in

COLOR A
✎ x4 3½in squares

COLOR B
✎ x4 1½in x 3½in

COLOR A
3½in   3½in   3½in   3½in

COLOR B
1½in x3½in

BACKGROUND
2½in x3½in

3½in x7½in

ASSEMBLE THE BLOCKS

✎ Sew a 1½in x 3½in accent rectangle to each 2½in x 3½in white rectangle.

✎ Sew a 1½in x 3½in accent rectangle to both sides of each 3½in x 7½in white rectangle.

✎ Sew the quilt block together in rows as shown.

✎ Repeat for all 42 quilt blocks.

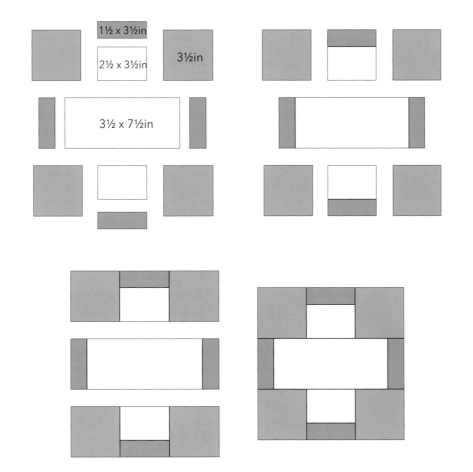

69

ASSEMBLE THE QUILT TOP

✎ If using ombre fabrics, arrange light to dark on a diagonal.

✎ Sew a 1½in x 9½in sashing piece to each block except the end of the row.

✎ Sew quilt top rows together.

✎ Sew the 1½in sashing strips together end to end. Measure the row and cut to width. Should be 59½in.

✎ Sew sashing in between rows.

✎ Sew 2½in x WOF borders together end to end. Measure the row and cut to width. Should be 59½in. Measure the length and cut to width. Should be 73½in.

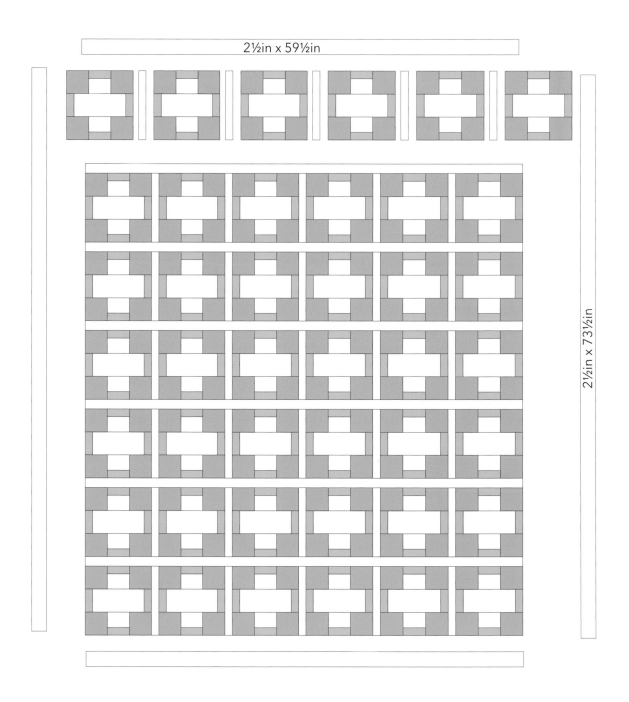

2½in x 59½in

2½in x 73½in

Shine On

Shine On

This small square throw is made up of bold and colorful blocks set on point. Choose a pop of color as your center accent piece to pull the blocks together. Shine on uses just twelve fat quarters mixed and matched to make up twelve blocks.

THROW SIZE
56IN X 56IN
12 BLOCKS | 12IN BLOCK

MATERIAL REQUIREMENTS

- ✎ **Solid Fabrics** x12 Fat Quarters
- ✎ **White Fabric** 1⅝ yards
- ✎ **Binding Fabric** ½ yard
- ✎ **Backing** 3⅝ yard
- ✎ **Batting** 64in x64in

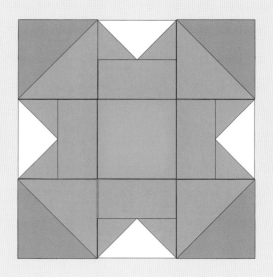

CUTTING INSTRUCTIONS

FROM EACH FAT QUARTER

- ✎ Cut x1 4½in square
- ✎ Cut x4 2½in x 4½in
- ✎ Cut x2 7in squares
- ✎ Cut x4 2⅞in squares

FROM BINDING FABRIC

- ✎ Cut x6 2½in x WOF strips

FROM THE WHITE FABRIC

- ✎ Cut x1 19in x WOF

  Subcut x2 19in squares
- ✎ Cut x1 14½in x WOF

  Subcut x2 14½in squares
- ✎ Cut x2 5¼in x WOF

  Subcut x12 5¼in squares
- ✎ Cut x6 1¾in x WOF

  Subcut x8 1¾in x 12½in

Set aside remaining for sashing

FAT QUARTER

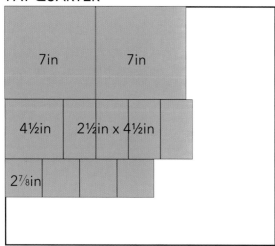

MIX AND MATCH THE FABRICS

✎ Mix and Match the pieces for each block.
Each block needs the following fabric cuts:

BACKGROUND	COLOR A	COLOR B	COLOR C
✎ x1 5¼in square	✎ x1 4½in square	✎ x4 2½in x 4½in	✎ x1 7in square
		✎ x1 7in square	
		✎ x4 2⅞ in squares	

BACKGROUND — 5¼in

COLOR A — 4½in

2½in x 4½in

COLOR A

2⅞in 2⅞in 2⅞in 2⅞in

COLOR C — 7in 7in

MAKE THE HALF SQUARE TRIANGLES FOUR AT A TIME

7in 7in

✎ Make the half square triangles four at a time.

✎ Place a 7in (B) square and a 7in (C) square right sides together. Pin in place and sew ¼in around the square.

✎ Cut the sewn unit on each diagonal.

✎ Press half square triangles open. Press seams open or towards the darker fabric.

✎ Trim half square triangles to 4½in square.

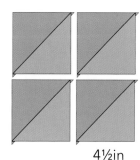

4½in

MAKE THE FLYING GEESE FOUR AT A TIME

✎ Mark a diagonal line on the wrong side of each 2⅞in (B) square.

✎ Place two 2⅞8in squares RST on the 5¼in background square as shown lining up the marked line.

✎ Sew ¼in from both sides of the marked line.

✎ Cut on the marked line.

✎ Flip corners up and press to form two heart shapes.

✎ Place a 2⅞in square on each heart unit as shown.

✎ Sew ¼in from both sides of the marked line.

✎ Cut on the marked line.

✎ Press the flying geese units open.

✎ Trim to 2½in x 4½in.

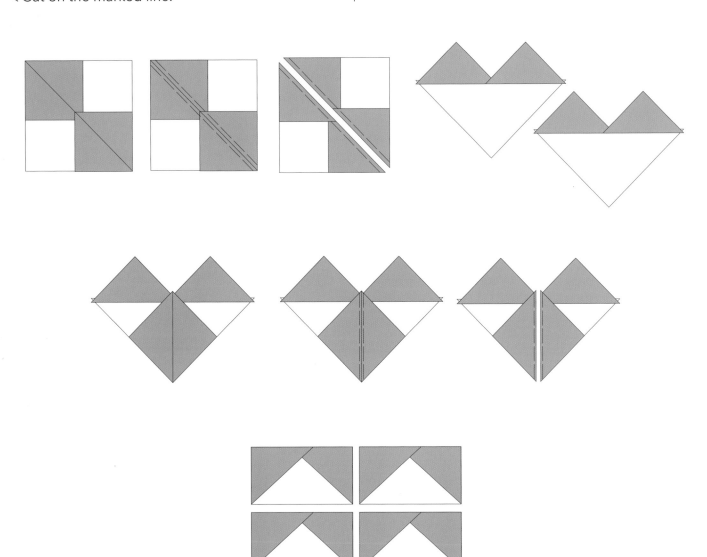

2½in x 4½in

ASSEMBLE THE BLOCKS

✎ Sew together the 2½in x 4½in flying geese units and the 2½in x 4½in (B) rectangles.

✎ Sew the quilt block together in rows.

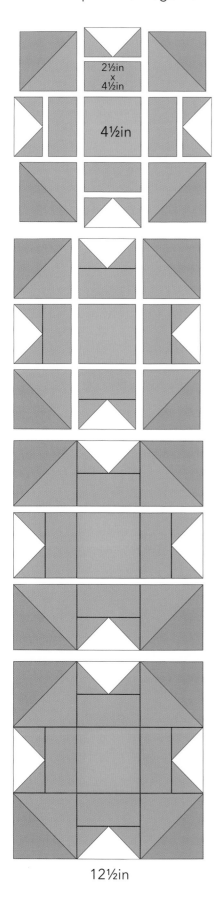

2½in
x
4½in

4½in

12½in

ASSEMBLE THE QUILT TOP

✎ This quilt goes together on point. Arrange the quilt blocks as shown.

✎ Cut the background 19in squares and the background 14½in squares on the diagonal. These are the setting triangles.

✎ Add 1¾in x 12½in sashing between blocks as shown.

✎ Sew together all of the remaining sashing WOF strips end to end. Cut the following row lengths: x2 25¾in and x1 52¼in.

✎ Sew Row one together. Add sashing to the bottom of the row. Sew the 14½in setting triangles to each side as shown.

✎ Sew row two together adding sashing between blocks.

✎ Sew row three together adding sashing between blocks.

✎ Sew rows two and three together adding the sashing between the row.

✎ Sew the 19in setting triangles to each side of the unit.

✎ Sew row four together adding the sashing to the top of the row. Sew the 14½in setting triangles to each side of the row as shown.

✎ Add the top and bottom setting triangles as shown.

✎ Trim quilt top square.

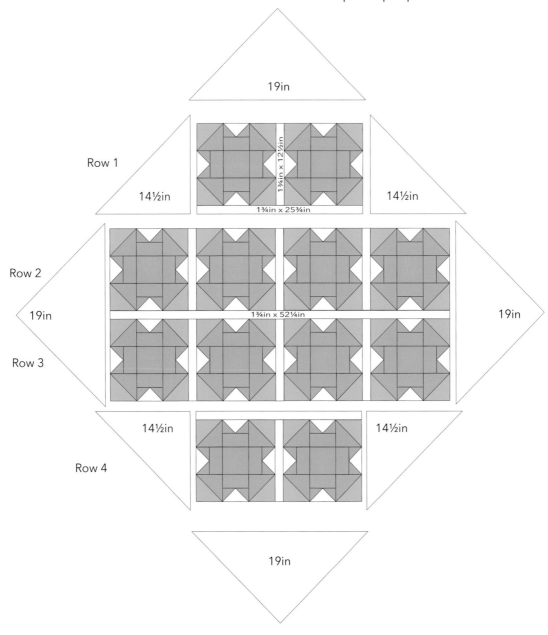

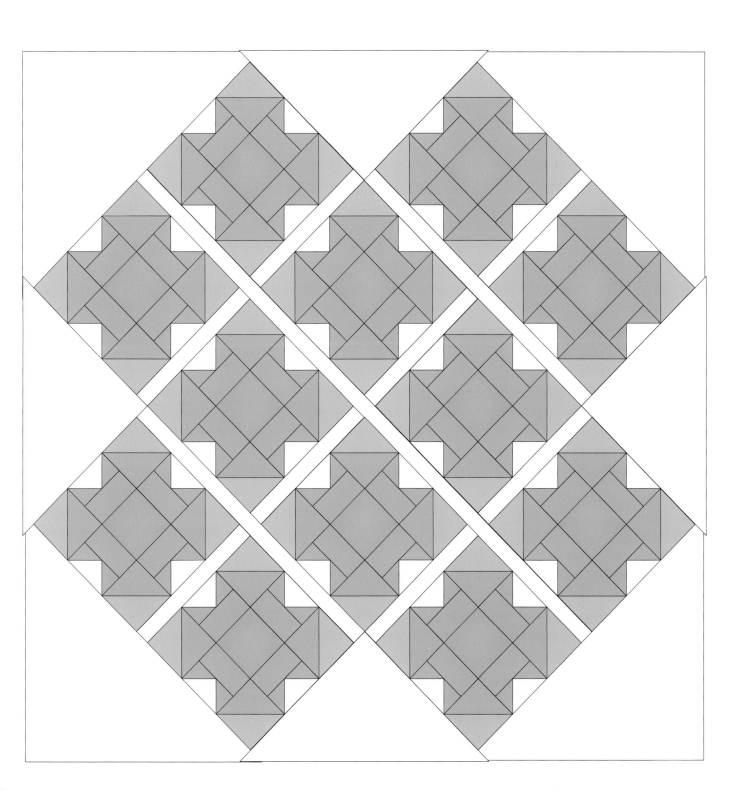

Sideways Arrows

Sideways Arrows is a fast and easy throw size quilt using the simple arrow shape. Use the four at a time flying geese method for quick construction. Choose an accent to go with your favorite fat eighths or grab some fabrics from your scrap stash to make up this modern arrow quilt.

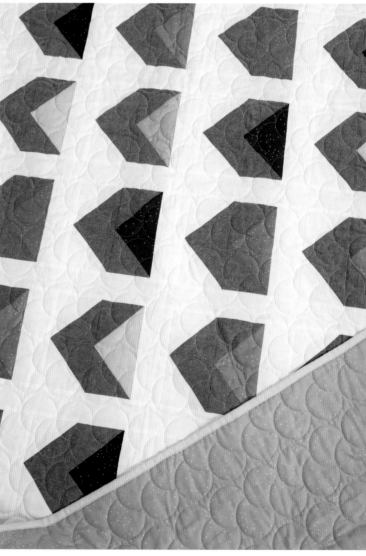

THROW SIZE
50IN X 66IN
48 BLOCKS | 6IN BLOCK

MATERIAL REQUIREMENTS

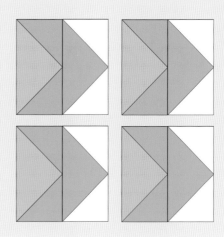

- Solid Fabrics x6 Fat Eighths
- Accent Fabric 1¼ yards
- White Fabric 2⅛ yards
- Binding Fabric ⅝ yards
- Backing 3¼ yards
- Batting 58in x 74in

CUTTING INSTRUCTIONS

FROM EACH FAT EIGHTH FABRIC

- Cut x2 7¼in squares

FROM THE ACCENT FABRIC

- Cut x3 7¼in x WOF

Subcut x12 7¼in squares

- Cut x5 3⅞in x WOF

Subcut x48 3⅞in squares

FROM BINDING FABRIC

- Cut x7 2½in x WOF strips

FROM THE WHITE FABRIC

- Cut x5 3⅞in x WOF

Subcut x48 3⅞in squares

- Cut x3 6½in x WOF

Subcut x40 2½in x 6½in

- Cut x14 2½in x WOF

Set aside for sashing and borders

FAT EIGHTH

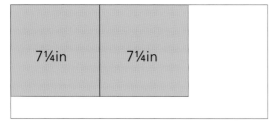

7¼in   7¼in

84

Each block needs the following fabric cuts (Makes Four):

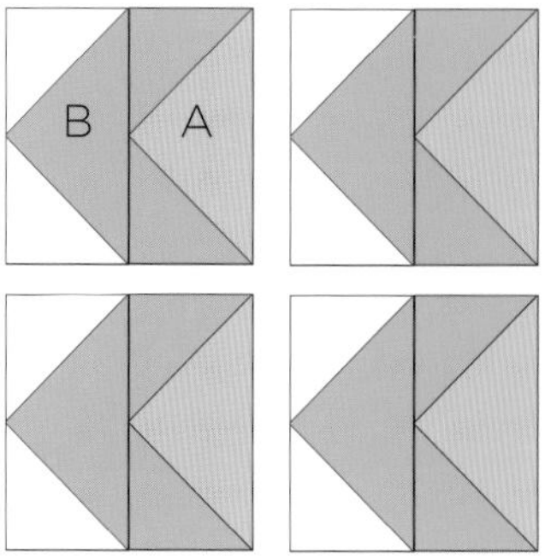

BACKGROUND
🪡 x4 3⅞in squares

COLOR A
🪡 x1 7¼ square

COLOR B
🪡 x4 3⅞in squares
🪡 x1 7¼in square

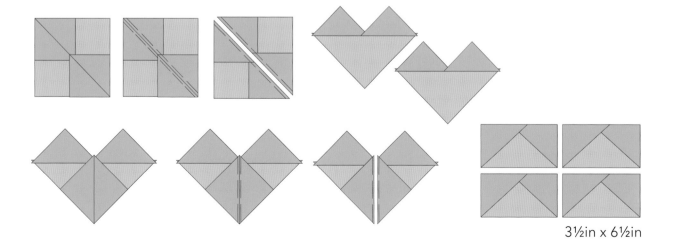

BACKGROUND	COLOR A	COLOR B (ACCENT)

3⅞in	3⅞in
3⅞in	3⅞in

COLOR A — 7¼in

COLOR B (ACCENT) — 7¼in

3⅞in	3⅞in
3⅞in	3⅞in

MAKE FLYING GEESE - FOUR AT A TIME

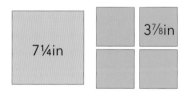

7¼in

3⅞in

🪡 Mark a diagonal line on the wrong side of each 3⅞in (B) square.

🪡 Place two 3⅞in squares RST on the 7¼in (A) square as shown lining up the marked line.

🪡 Sew ¼in from both sides of the marked line.

🪡 Cut on the marked line.

🪡 Flip corners up and press to form two heart shapes.

🪡 Place a 3⅞in square on each heart unit as shown.

🪡 Sew ¼in from both sides of the marked line.

🪡 Cut on the marked line.

🪡 Press the flying geese units open.

🪡 Trim to 3½in x 6½in.

🪡 Repeat using all color (A) 7¼in squares and 3⅞in accent squares. Makes 8 flying geese of each color.

3½in x 6½in

Repeat using the 7¼in (B) and the four 3⅞ background squares. Make 48 flying geese units.

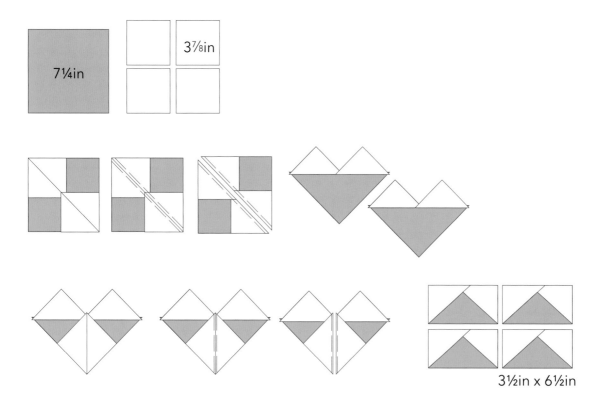

ASSEMBLE THE BLOCKS

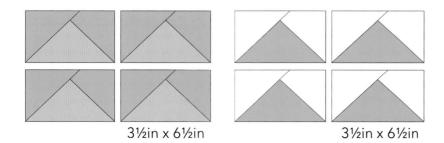

3½in x 6½in   3½in x 6½in

Sew the flying geese together to make each block. Makes four blocks.

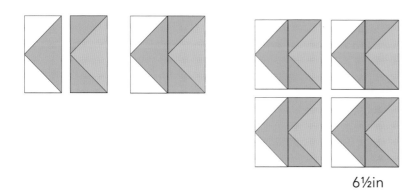

6½in

ASSEMBLE THE QUILT TOP

✎ Arrange the quilt blocks in eight rows of six. Add 2½in x 6½in sashing pieces between blocks.

✎ Sew together all of the sashing WOF strips end to end. Cut to each row length of 46½in.

✎ Sew rows together adding the sashing in between each row and the top and the bottom.

✎ Cut the side sashing to 66½in. Attach to both sides.

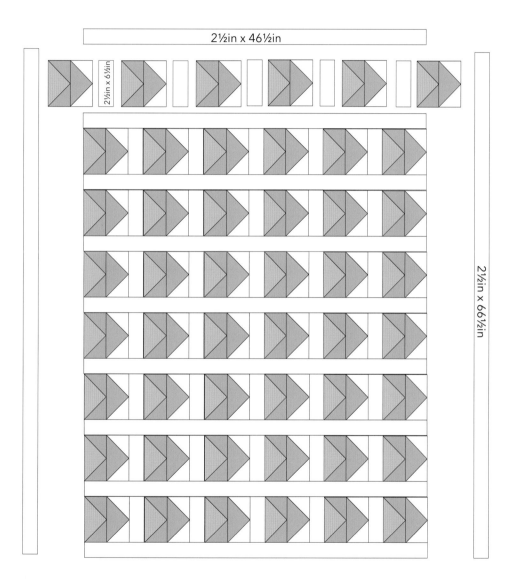

Tiled Stars

Tiled Stars is a generous throw size quilt inspired from ceramic tiling. The intricate design makes for a unique star quilt. Use just ten fat quarters mixed and matched to create this quilt.

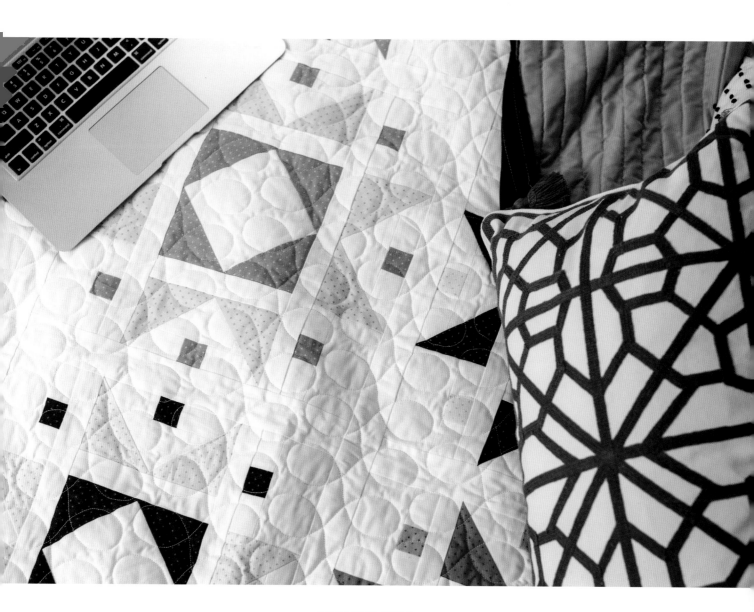

THROW SIZE
63IN X 79IN
20 BLOCKS | 14IN BLOCK

MATERIAL REQUIREMENTS

- ✎ **Solid Fabrics** x10 fat quarters
- ✎ **White Fabric** 5¼ yards
- ✎ **Binding Fabric** ⅔ yard
- ✎ **Backing** 4⅞ yard
- ✎ **Batting** 71in x 87in

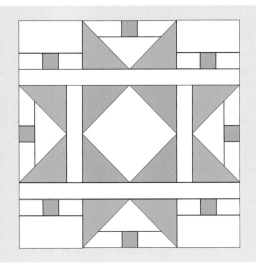

CUTTING INSTRUCTIONS

FROM EACH FAT QUARTER

- ✎ Cut x4 3⅞in squares
- ✎ Cut x16 1½in squares
- ✎ Cut x16 3½in squares

FROM BINDING FABRIC

- ✎ Cut x8 2½in x WOF strips

FROM THE WHITE FABRIC

- ✎ Cut x3 14½in x WOF

From 2 strips subcut x40 1½in x 14½in

From 1 strip subcut x15 2in x 14½in

- ✎ Cut x7 6½in x WOF

From 2 strips, subcut x40 1½in x 6½in

From 5 strips, subcut x80 2½in x 6½in

- ✎ Cut x3 4¾in x WOF

Subcut x20 4¾in squares

- ✎ Cut x5 4½in x WOF

Subcut x80 2½in x 4½in

- ✎ Cut x6 3in x WOF

Subcut x160 1½in x 3in

- ✎ Cut x6 2in x WOF

Subcut x160 1½in x 2in

- ✎ Cut x13 2in x WOF

Set aside for sashing

FAT QUARTER 21IN X 18IN

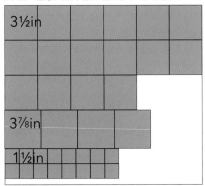

3½in

3⅞in

1½in

Makes 2 blocks

90

MIX AND MATCH THE FABRICS FOR EACH BLOCK

✎ Mix and Match the pieces for each block.
Each block needs the following fabric cuts:

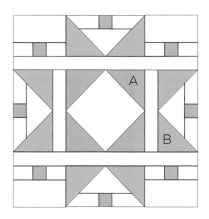

BACKGROUND

- ✎ x8-1½in x 3in
- ✎ x8-1½in x 2in
- ✎ x4-2½in x 4½in
- ✎ x4-2½in x 6½in
- ✎ x2-1½in x 6½in
- ✎ x2-1½in x 14½in
- ✎ x1-4¾in squares

COLOR A

- ✎ x2-3⅞in squares
- ✎ x8-1½in squares

COLOR B

- ✎ x8-3½in squares

BACKGROUND

1½in x 3in   2½in x 4½in   1½in x 6½in   1½in x 14½in

4¾in

2½in x 6½in

1½in x 2in

COLOR A

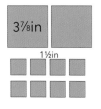

3⅞in

1½in

COLOR B

3½in 3½in 3½in 3½in

3½in 3½in 3½in 3½in

MAKE THE CENTER SQUARE IN A SQUARE

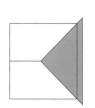

4¾in   3⅞in

✎ Make the center square in a square unit using one 4¾in background square and the two 3⅞in color A squares.

✎ Cut the 3⅞in squares on the diagonal to create four triangles.

✎ Sew the cut triangles to each side of the 4¾in background square. Fold the square in half to create a crease down the middle. Line the tip of the triangle up with the crease line for a perfectly centered unit.

✎ Trim the edges straight.

✎ Repeat on the other side.

✎ Trim to 6½in square leaving at least ¼in between each point and the edge for the seam allowance.

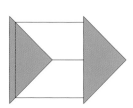
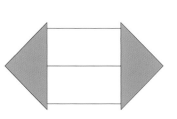
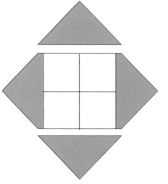
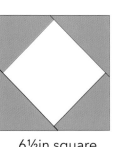

6½in square

MAKE THE CORNER UNITS

🪡 Sew together a background 1½in x 2in rectangle to a 1½in (A) square and another 1½in x 2in background rectangle.

🪡 Press seams outwards.

🪡 Sew a background 2½in x 4½in rectangle to each of these units.

🪡 Make 4 units per block.

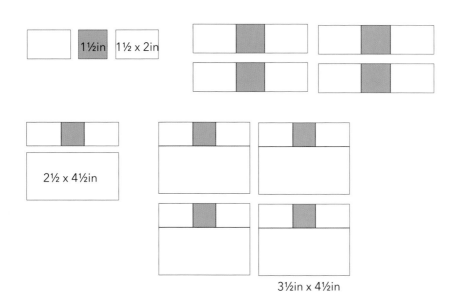

3½in x 4½in

MAKE THE FLYING GEESE UNITS

🪡 Sew together a background 1½in x 3in rectangle to a 1½in (A) square and another background 1½in x 3in rectangle.

🪡 Press seams outwards.

🪡 Sew a background 2½in x 6½in rectangle to each of these units.

🪡 Make 4 units per block.

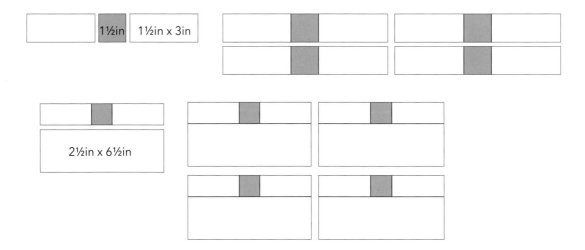

Mark a diagonal line on the wrong side of each 3½in (B) square.

Place the 3½in square RST on the pieced 3½in x 6½in unit as shown.

Sew on the marked line.

Trim ¼in from the marked line.

Flip corner open and press.

Repeat for the other corner.

Make four flying geese units per block.

   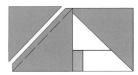 

ASSEMBLE THE BLOCKS

Arrange the units as shown below.

Sew the rows together adding the 1½in x 6½in sashing as shown.

Add the 1½in x 14½in sashing between the rows and sew block together.

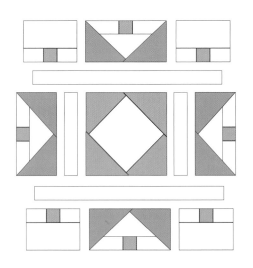 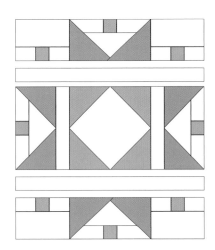 

14½in square

ASSEMBLE THE QUILT TOP

✎ Arrange the quilt blocks in five rows of four. Add 2in x 14½in sashing pieces between blocks.

✎ Sew together all of the sashing WOF strips end to end. Cut to each row length of 60½in.

✎ Sew rows together adding the sashing in between each row and the top and the bottom.

✎ Cut the side sashing to 79½in. Attach to both sides.

2½in x 60½in

2½in x 79½in

Block by Block Sampler

Make up this fun and modern sampler by sewing together each of the eleven blocks in this book. Make it bold and colorful or choose your favorite prints. Make test blocks of each quilt and use them for this sampler as a bonus project.

THROW SIZE
60IN X 66IN

MATERIAL REQUIREMENTS

✎ **11 completed blocks** (x2 Sideways Arrows)

✎ **White Fabric** 1½ yards

✎ **Binding Fabric** ⅝ yard

✎ **Backing** 4 yards

✎ **Batting** 68in x 74in

CUTTING INSTRUCTIONS

FROM THE WHITE FABRIC

✎ Cut x7 3½in x WOF

Sew together end to end and subcut:

✎ x1 3½in x 17½in

✎ x1 3½in x 32½in

✎ x2 3½in x 55½in

✎ x2 3½in x 66½in

✎ Cut x7 2½in x WOF

Sew together end to end and subcut:

✎ x3 2½in x 12½in

✎ x1 2½in x 18½in

✎ x2 2½in x 24½in

✎ x4 2½in x 6½in

✎ x4 2½in x 14½in

✎ x1 2½in x 15½in

✎ x2 2½in x 4½in

✎ x1 2½in x 60½in

✎ Cut x1 2in x WOF

Subcut x2 2in x 10½in

✎ Cut x1 1½in x WOF

Subcut x1 1½in x 14½in

Subcut x1 1½in x 9½in

Subcut x1 1½in x 4½in

✎ Cut x1 5¼in x WOF

Subcut x4 5¼in squares for hourglass units

FROM BINDING FABRIC

✎ Cut x7 2½in x WOF strips

FROM ADDITIONAL SOLID OR PRINT FABRICS

✎ Cut x4 5¼in squares

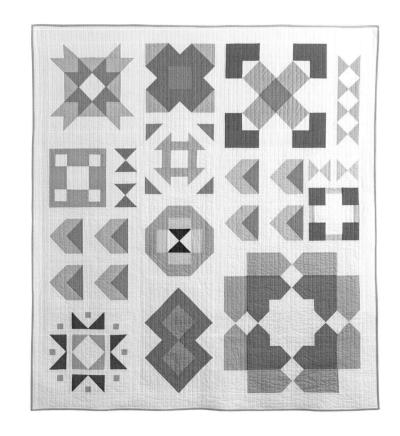

MAKE THE HOURGLASSES

The sampler quilt needs an additional eight 4½in hourglass blocks.

✎ Make the hourglass units using one 5¼in background square and one 5¼in solid or print square.

✎ Place the squares RST.

✎ Mark a diagonal on the wrong side of the fabric.

✎ Sew ¼in away from the marked line on each side.

✎ Cut on the marked line.

✎ Press the units open towards the darker fabric.

✎ Place the two half square triangles right sides together in opposite directions. The seams should nest.

✎ Mark a line on the diagonal that's perpindicular to the seam line. Pin in place to prevent shifting.

✎ Sew ¼in on each side of the drawn line.

✎ Cut on the marked line.

✎ Press units open.

✎ Trim to 4½in.

✎ Repeat four times for a total of eight hourglass units.

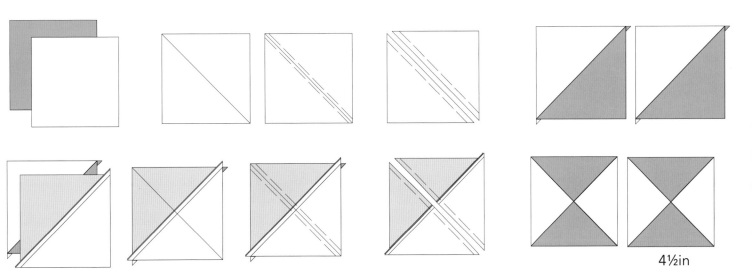

4½in

ASSEMBLE THE QUILT TOP

✎ Assemble the quilt top in sections adding sashing as shown.

✎ Add the top and bottom border.

✎ Add the side borders.

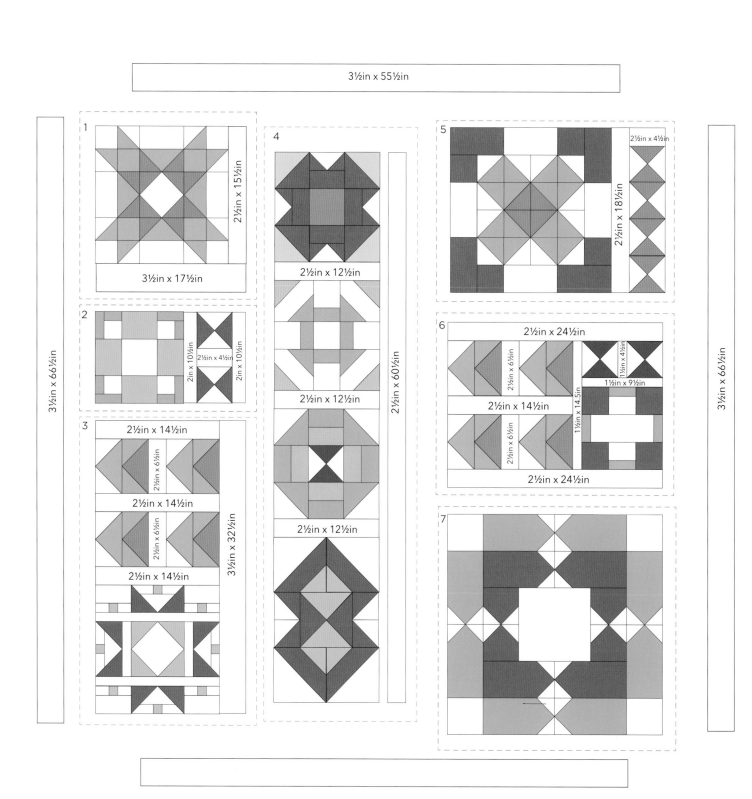

FABRIC CREDITS

01 CHURN DASH

Prints - Mixed fat quarter bundle from Stash Fabrics

White - Robert Kaufman

Binding - Riley Blake provided by Simply Macbeth Design Co.

Backing - Intermix by Dear Stella Design

Quilted by Kaitlyn Howell

#bbbchurndash

02 FIGURE EIGHTS

Prints - Wink by Birch Fabrics

White - Robert Kaufman

Backing - Birch Fabrics

Quilted by Kaitlyn Howell

#bbbFigureeights

03 FIRST PLACE

Prints - Yukatan by Moda Fabrics

Aqua Solids - Moda Fabrics

White - Robert Kaufman

Binding - Timeless Treasures

Backing - Moda Fabrics

Quilted by Kaitlyn Howell

#bbbfirstplace

04 HOPSCOTCH

Prints - Bake Shop by Michael Miller Fabrics

Accent - Yarn Dyed Essex Linen by Robert Kaufman in Black

White - Robert Kaufman

Backing and Binding - Cotton and Steel

Quilted by Emily Dennis

#bbbhopscotch

05 HOURGLASS

Prints - Mixed fat quarter bundle by ilovefabric

Hourglass Solid - Mediterranean by Robert Kaufman

Accent - Yarn Dyed Essex Linen by Robert Kaufman in Graphite

White - Robert Kaufman

Backing - Daisy Chain by Wyndham Fabrics

Quilted by Kaitlyn Howell

#bbbhourglass

06 KRISS CROSS

Solids - Robert Kaufman

Binding - Silver by Robert Kaufman

Backing - Trellis by Robert Kaufman

Quilted by Emily Dennis

#bbbkrisscross

07 MINI MEDALLION

Prints - To Market by Cloud 9 Fabrics

Solids - Robert Kaufman in Mediterranean

Accent - Essex Linen by Robert Kaufman

Quilted by Emily Dennis

#bbbminiquilt

08 OMBRE SQUARES

Prints - Confetti Ombre by Moda Fabrics

Stripes - Timeless Treasures

White - Robert Kaufman

Binding- Silver by Robert Kaufman

Backing - Moda Fabrics

Quilted by Kaitlyn Howell

#bbbOmbreSquares

9 SHINE ON

Prints - Speckles by Cotton & Steel

White - Cotton Couture by RJR

Binding - Cotton & Steel

Backing - Cotton & Steel

Quilted by Kaitlyn Howell

#bbbShineOn

10 SIDEWAYS ARROWS

Prints - Basics by Cotton & Steel

Accent - Yarn Dyed Essex Linen by Robert Kaufman

Binding - Silver by Robert Kaufman

Backing - Basics by Cotton & Steel

Quilted by Kaitlyn Howell

#bbbsidewaysarrows

11 TILED STARS

Prints - Basics by Cotton & Steel

White - Kona Cotton by Robert Kaufman

Binding - Basics by Cotton & Steel

Backing - Basics by Cotton & Steel

Quilted by Kaitlyn Howell

#bbbtiledstars

12 BLOCK BY BLOCK SAMPLER

Solids - Robert Kaufman

Backing- Intermix by Dear Stella Design

Quilted by Emily Dennis

#bbbsamplerquilt

All quilts pieced on a Janome MC6700p sewing machine.